Jersey nursing homes – off-
d long-term care facilities – at
residents have died from the
25% all COVID-19-relat-

show a lon
ad nursing

demic outbreak
deadly consequences. One
troublesome – but frequent
of problems in the nursing
industry across the nation. Keep
ents safe from germs.
"The best nursing homes
difficulty dealing with COVID
akes you look to see if the en
is in need of change," said Al
n associate professor of nu
field, University in Conne
research focuses on
issues have been compil
es' policy: Nursing homes
to take back residents wi
s or take in new patien

. Andrew Cuomo said if
can't handle an infected
need to call the state to
transferred. The
hed an investigation in
s to ensure they are foll
es.
he nursing home can
p a patient if they can
e care for that patie
Monday.
they have COVID p
D patient, but they
uate care for that patie
ation to transfer, the
n Monday. Westche
it would test all patie
omes, where 284 pe
6% of the total dea
nty.
ed
we can."
All it takes is one p
nursing home w**ole system'**
n you're off to t

We're doing everyth
ressor for the wh

Foreword

Everyone deserves a happy ending, whether it's at a wedding or a funeral. The problem is — life.

By night, I write Regency-era romances. By day, I officiate at weddings and funerals as a rabbi. The two parts of my life, like this book, are oddly compatible. The feelings evoked by both life cycle events — weddings and funerals — are oddly similar. Except that there are often more laughs at funerals and more tears at weddings.

My dear friend, James W. Gaynor, has brilliantly captured this paradox in his lovely collection of poems that reflect on the human condition at the best and worst times of our lives. (And don't fall into the trap of thinking that weddings are the best!)

20 Poems Inappropriate for a Wedding

Jim, who has never been married and so probably has a clearer understanding of marital bliss than those of us who are or have been, deftly skewers our ideas about what marriage is all about in his collection of inappropriate poems for weddings. Take, for example, his view of marital fidelity in "Garden of Matrimony:"

> "Whenever you weren't here
>   you were horizontal
>   entwining in someone else's Eden."

I love his radical feminist understanding of marriage, highlighted in the hilarious "The Museum of Hideous Bridesmaid Dresses:"

> "In this building
> white
> does not signal surrender."

And who could deny the truth of his poem that reflects on why there is an absence of blenders as wedding gifts at a wedding between two people who marry later in life in the appropriately titled, "An Absence of Blenders?"

> "As if everyone present has agreed
> a machine with a lifetime warranty is
> an outdated cultural artifact"

This collection of poems about the joys and perils of weddings and the marital state will give the happily married a reason to be smug, and those on the brink of committing marriage some disturbing dreams.

Happy reading!

Nola Saint James

nolasaintjames.com

Contents

Chalking It Up to Experience Requires Chalk 11

    It Happens Unexpectedly 13

    Rethinking the Guest List 15

    Falcon Yard 17

    Garden of Matrimony 19

    Vortex 21

Regrets Require Storage Space 23

    Marital Flight Patterns 25

    Health Advisory 27

    Inevitably Morning Happens 29

    Surface Tension 31

    The Museum of Hideous Bridesmaid Dresses 33

    An Absence of Blenders 37

    Macbeth for Adulterers 39

All That Unspoken Hope 41

    Jailbreak 43

Independence Day 45

Reassessment Vows 47

After the Reception 49

Fairy Tale 51

You Never Know **53**

Wedding Toast 55

Personal Possessions 57

Marketing 101 59

Viking Prenup 61

Some Assembly Required 63

Introduction + More About Author **64**

Chalking It Up to Experience Requires Chalk

It Happens Unexpectedly

you begin to wonder what you'll wear
to the funeral of your spouse —
who's happily alive in the next room

sunglasses definitely
a religious service for an atheist
as a final nod to the in-laws with whom
you'll never have to share another holiday meal
how soon before finding a new home
for the cat you've always hated, going online
in search of frequent no-strings sex, and marrying
yet another version of your problematic parent

but then you hear a familiar something —
his voice, her laugh, their sneeze —
and now it's time for dinner

Rethinking the Guest List

Centaurs have a history
of regrettable behavior at weddings
particularly when
there's an open bar and
the stallion self reawakens to an
embarrassment of chiffon
not to mention the pungent scent —
unavoidable under the circumstances —
of the occasional usher

Falcon Yard
[for Ted Hughs and Sylvia Plath]

All the biting and the blood
two predators mating
deep in the dark February forest
of 1956 Cambridge
would later be a clue*
somehow someone but who
would not get out alive

---

* In Point of Fact

    There are reasons
    why everyone should
    think twice before
    adoring a Fascist.

Garden of Matrimony

Unseen movement heard
in ginger kinking vines
sidewinding reminding me

Whenever you weren't here
you were horizontal
entwining in someone else's Eden

Vortex

Mistakes were made
and you find yourself
a noun without a verb form

a blinded deer first surprised
then swirled into a headlight-lit
cyclone too late a warning
of imminent collision
with the semi your future ex is driving

Regrets Require Storage Space

Marital Flight Patterns

The peacock can fly but not well
the peahen does better but not much
sufficient to find a branch high enough
to thwart night-hunting foxes
yet nowhere near what's needed
to challenge owls in mid-swoop.

And there we have it — both genders can fly
but not to great height nor for a distance
that could qualify them for reclassification
out of the exotic into the migratory.

Health Advisory

Words from the wise to those not yet so:

>Wearing your heart on your sleeve
>or on any part of your clothing
>may well interfere with cardiac function
>likely resulting in death.

Inevitably Morning Happens

I awake reborn as someone
I really don't want to know
ill-tempered
capable of kicking the cat
in homicidal need of coffee

You've been up for some time
determined
to make both the bed and a difference
never resenting the necessity
of brushing your teeth

Which among other reasons
is why we now
have separate bedrooms
located
in different coastal time zones

Surface Tension

Water isn't wet, but it creates wet,
a side effect of molecular interaction
between occasional discrete entities,
which is dried, over time,
by the process of evaporation.

Not unlike love, which also creates wet,
a side effect of molecular interaction
between occasional discrete entities,
which is dried, over time,
creating scarring on heart tissue.

The Museum of Hideous Bridesmaid Dresses

The museum is a popular weekend tourist destination currently featuring: "Chiffon and Sun Tzu's The Art of War."

Military action is the path
of life and death for every nation
and worthy of study.
— "Strategic Assessments"

The entry fee includes a guided tour
led by a lieutenant colonel (ret.)
who most recently occupied Iraq.

Destroy the energy
of the enemy's armies
by killing their generals' hearts.
— "Armed Struggle"

This collection proves
in sickness and in health
no one ever looked good wearing orange.

Those who triumph
without fighting
are the true champions.
  — "Planning a Siege"

A designer explosion in violent green
demonstrates how bankrupting one's attendants
is an effective way to maintain control.

The most important characteristic
of any military action
is not persistence but victory.
  — "Doing Battle"

In this building
white
does not signal surrender.

An Absence of Blenders

One wonderful thing among many
about later-in-life weddings
is an absence of blenders

As if everyone present has agreed
a machine with a lifetime warranty
is an outdated cultural artifact

Macbeth for Adulterers

The time we spent so long ago
betraying our respective mates
was an interlude neither of us remembers
as earthshaking yet ever since
in good times and bad
in sickness and health
both richer and poorer
at gatherings where we now meet
our bespoke ghost takes a comfortable chair
flashing his now-familiar grin
and looks around to see who else he knows

All That Unspoken Hope

Jailbreak

Marriage isn't always the prison
that dare not speak its name
but once the bars begin to scream
it's time to get the hell out

Let me be
    the file hidden in the cake
    the toothbrush now a shiv
    the tunnel to your new life

Because orange is most definitely
not your color and yes
that jumpsuit makes you look fat
start digging

Independence Day

The deed of transfer was the least among
today's historic documents,
establishing a day of remembrance
we'll both celebrate — separately —
for years to come.

But suddenly it was all
*whatarewedoing whatarewedoing
whatwerewethinking* — and although
Jefferson and the other wigs may well
have asked themselves the same
questions — later answered in
monuments, currency and a national holiday —
at some point they probably
shrugged their shoulders and said,
whatthehell whatthehell —
Let's just get it over with and sign the damned paper.

Reassessment Vows

You're not the person
I thought you were
but then again
who I thought you were
isn't who you are now either
never was and won't ever be.

As it turns out
I'm not who I thought I was
but then again (again)
the person I thought I was
isn't who I am now either
never was and won't ever be

Therefore dearly beloved
for better or worse
etc. etc. etc.
until death us do part
this is who we are
so we'd better get used to it.

After the Reception

We could not have known then
how it would play out
but we all agreed about the salmon

Fairy Tale

Once upon a time

hiding skeletons in the closet
knowing where the bodies are buried
adding insult to injury
were figurative phrases

or so I thought
but in our story
they were not
making it impossible to

live happily ever after

You Never Know

Wedding Toast
(in absentia)

I without question remain
among the uninvited
a status I ascribe to
the happy couple's irrational fear
that along with the granular good wishes
some rice pudding might get thrown

Which now that I think of it
is not so very farfetched
and quite probably why my absence
is not such a bad thing
at this long-delayed second wedding
of my two former spouses

Personal Possessions

When I was younger
a lover was
let's say a wallet
susceptible to theft
sometimes misplaced and
later found in another pocket
maybe mine

Today
a husband is
let's say a different accessory
necessary on occasion
frequently lost but
nobody steals
reading glasses

Marketing 101

Our limited shelf life
distribution issues and
lack of child-proof packaging
should have indicated
more market research
prior to our brand launch
was necessary.

But a greater understanding
of our limited shelf life
distribution issues and
lack of child-proof packaging
would not have changed
that you and I were
broccoli-flavored toothpaste.

Viking Prenup

I am a day at the beach
but neither the sun nor sugary sand
bordering plowable land you are

I am a fjord
jagged rocks overcast with distant thunder
and when my pillaging is done

I will leave as I have come
taking as much of value
as I can carry

Some Assembly Required

This ceremony
seemed to call for
a celebratory sonnet —
a 14-line RDA of
similes and iambs,
knit together by
an overarching
central metaphor
about the
fleeting nature of
love, existence and
the weather.

But, as in poetry, life;
I was mistaken.

Copyright© 2024 by James W. Gaynor. All rights reserved.
ISBN 978-0-9978428-7-6
Designed by: Kelly Duke McKinley, theshopkeys.com
NemetonPress@gmail.com, 240 E 76 St., 15W, New York, NY 10021

For Jo and Nola, with deepest love from their J. Willy

Introduction

"Poetry is most often experienced unintentionally at private ceremonies such as weddings and funerals, with eighty percent of the potential audience and more than ninety percent of the current audience reporting that they've been exposed to poetry at one of these private occasions."

— Poetry in America Study commissioned by the Poetry Foundation

"The choice of what to read at a ritual requiring poetry can be daunting. In recognition of that fact, this collection aspires to be helpful in identifying some poems best read before or after — but not actually at — the ceremony in question. Knowing what not to say is always a good first step."

— James W. Gaynor

About the Authors

Photo Credit: Justin Wilson

James W. Gaynor is the author of *I'll Miss You Later* and *Jane Austen's Pride and Prejudice in 61 Haiku*. On occasion, he has been asked to write and/or read a poem for a wedding or a funeral. None of the poems in this collection made the cut.

Nola Saint James writes stirring Recency- era romance novels featuring heroines who contrive to save themselves and the men who love them.
nolasaintjames.com

Rabbi Dr. Jo David specializes in teaching the Bible as literature and performs lifecycle ceremonies for Jewish and interfaith families.
rabbijodavid.com

PS: About the Porn

If you're reading this,
you've opened the box and
now have met those special friends
about whom I never talked.

Please think of them as
inappropriately dressed mourners
you'll be spared meeting
at the funeral and reading of the will.

Although among them
there are a few favorites who
deserve some recognition for
their years of faithful service

La Traviata *for Dummies*

Once upon a Belle Époque
in an apartment well beyond her means
on the fashionable rue Gambetta
lived the beautiful Violetta

Her boyfriend's name was Alfredo
not even close friends called him Al
they fell in love though his father objected
then nothing went quite as expected

Vi was not well and Al not too bright
their overture was in E major
everyone knew sadly
it would all end badly

And it did

Natural History

Unlike familiar petrified skeletons —
lobe-finned fish and extinct giant parrots —
fossils at the Musée Curie
belong to an epoch neither named
nor past — and cannot be displayed.

The glowing tubes Marie carried in her pockets,
whose soft light she found enchanting,
eventually killed her — transforming
her notebooks into hazmat so dangerous
they are still entombed in lead-lined boxes.

Even her recipe collection is off limits —
and so, hidden deep within Radium's
millennial half-life, Mme. Curie's
rigorously tested formula for mayonnaise.
remains an archeological secret.

Five Stages of Death in the Morning

The ritual begins the night before
when the body is committed
to the bed in sure and certain hope
of resurrection in the morning

Waking to an alarm clock-based liturgy of:
    Denial
    Anger
    Bargaining
    Depression
    Acceptance
involving frequent use
of the snooze button

The five stages of death in the morning
sure and certain until the inevitable
but so far so good
we're not dead yet

Another Way To Go

In the half-light end-of-day dimness
preceding nightly death
when the diem has been carpe-d and
unanchored with each breath

Alternative endings appear
for ghostly stories not our own
but lived and died, and told / retold
a form of bedtime koan

Medea decided good riddance
Juliet chose rueful laughter
Diana got out of the car
and they all lived happily ever after

First, Get Dressed

Exit Lady Montague

Montague: Alas, my liege, my wife is dead to-night;
Grief of my son's exile hath stopp'd her breath:
What further woe conspires against mine age?

In a life lived mostly offstage
Lady Montague had three lines
no first name that we know of
and her only son was something of a disappointment

At least she was spared
finding out Juliet had become
her daughter-in-law
but that news would have killed her anyway

No Comment

It's your funeral
is something people will say
from time to time
throughout your life
but for obvious reasons
not when they're actually
at your funeral

Usually an Aunt

If a family is a complicated geography
with singular customs,
an undocumented language and
varying climate zones,

then someone —
usually an aunt —
becomes a trade-regulating waterway.

But borders shift, cities vanish
and rivers change course, leaving
mysterious remnants, so

then someone —
usually an aunt —
becomes a topographic map of last resort.

And when she's gone, it all disappears.

Final Cut

[♪]
At long last you are a collector's edition
deleted scenes restored
director commentaries
subtitles in three languages
and for the hearing-impaired
bracketed descriptions music-note symbols
announcing instrumental warnings [♪]
violin tremors whose ominous messages
you never seemed to hear
but which were clear
to those of us
your devoted fans
who are now gathered grieving

[muffled sobs] [♪]

Mesozoic Beliefs

Religious dinosaurs
were convinced the asteroid
was on its way but
they went on with
business as usual
grazing rampaging
building cathedrals of bone
for scriptural futures
in which they would be unknown

Condolence Email Template

Subject Line: Your recent loss

[NAME] is now living in our thoughts, among all our other dear — a few not quite so — departed.

But even spiritual arenas have a maximum capacity — and not all of this crowd got along with each other when they were here (you know who I mean).

So, let's be sad, but agree to keep only the living in our thoughts and forget [NAME] immediately.

Sincerely
[YOUR NAME]

I Now Sleep on Your Side of the Bed

Fun Ways to Grieve

Make a list
write down what you hated
and then
read it aloud
while smiling ruefully

Strike a match
light some candles
and then
humming softly
set the curtains on fire

Walk out the door
close it behind you
and then
from a distance
watch it all burn down

Change your name
leave the country
and then knowing
what you know
start over

A Better Question

What next
isn't the right question
when the funeral is over
because everyone knows
nobody knows for sure.

Now what
is a better question
when the funeral is over
because everyone knows
it's time to eat.

Return to Sender

There's no longer a month
something doesn't come due

a phantom reminder
you don't live here anymore

which I can't forward because
there's no postal service in hell

Hilter's Dog, Hemingway's Mother

Hitler (reportedly) loved
his dog, Blondi,
who (undoubtedly) loved him back,
e.g.,
on their last night together in the bunker,
she (immediately) swallowed the cyanide capsules
he gave her to make sure they would work for him.

Hemingway (reportedly) disliked
his mother, Grace,
who (undoubtedly) reciprocated,
e.g.,
when *The Sun Also Rises* was published,
she (immediately) told him every page
had filled her with a sick loathing.

All of which puts (absolutely) nothing
into perspective — except perhaps — that
adverbs and suicide are (usually) optional.

What Ends Badly
Doesn't Always Begin Badly

I Might As Well Live

Your memorial service has convened
a handsome demographic. all of whom
seem to share an unspoken knowledge
of your naked enthusiasm —

and now,
soundless communications —
glances usually exchanged elsewhere
at a much later hour — begin to mingle
with the grief and the coffee,

which
makes me think this would be a good time
to avoid your husband — we both know why –
and introduce myself to the smoldering leather jacket standing near
the door

I'll miss you later.

Rent-a-Tomb

My dream of being a famous jazz harpsichordist
has not yet come true but it lives
somewhere in Brooklyn in a self-storage unit
entombed among labeled boxes
of invented memories and sexual fantasies
stacked on top of a cardboard sarcophagus
containing an unfaithful lover's mummified corpse —
treasures until now undisturbed

In vs. On

Possibly due to rules governing prepositions
love or its absence is popular
in
poetry and suicide notes
yet rarely appears
on
to-do and shopping lists

To-Do List

Buy the flowers yourself
Start early
Take the dog
Consult your lawyers (again)
Ignore the mermaids
Become more dangerous
Remember the horrible mother
Forget about Proust in the original
Give the clothes to Goodwill
Get away with murder

Drop-in Phantoms

It's never easy when the dead return
as they do from time to time
uninvited but not unwelcome
except when they go on and on
about what could or should
have been different

despite knowing
it could only have been what it was
which is why they're dead

and you're not

Self-Awareness is a Glass of Unsweetened Lemonade

I Now Sleep On Your Side of the Bed ... 90

Condolence Email Template 88

Mesozoic Beliefs 86

Final Cut 84

Usually an Aunt 82

No Comment 80

Exit Lady Montague 78

First, Get Dressed ... 76

Another Way to Go 74

Five Stages of Death in the Morning 72

Natural History 70

La Traviata for Dummies 68

PS: About the Porn 66

Introduction + More About Author ... 65

Contents

Self-Awareness is a Glass of Unsweetened Lemonade..................112
    Drop-in Phantoms 110
    To-Do List.. 108
    In vs. On 106
    Rent-a-Tomb 104
    I Might as Well Live 102

What Ends Badly Doesn't Always Begin Badly..............................100
    Hitler's Dog, Hemingway's Mother...98
    Return to Sender 96
    A Better Question 94
    Fun Ways to Grieve 92

"Vi was not well and Al not too bright
 their overture was in E major
 everyone knew sadly
 it would all end badly
 And it did"

This collection of poems about the end of life and its aftermath will make you glad to be alive.

Happy reading!

— RABBI DR. JO DAVID

rabbijodavid.wordpress.com

Take, for example, his reflection on guests at a memorial service in "I Might As Well Live:"

> "soundless communications —
> glances usually exchanged elsewhere
> at a much later hour — begin to mingle
> with the grief and the coffee,"

The poem ends with a wonderful line, "I'll miss you later." This is the title of another of Jim's collections of poetry that deals with love and loss and hope,

His poem, *Usually an Aunt*, focuses on the phenomenon of generational loss in a way that is reminiscent of haiku — another poetic form at which Jim is adept. (See his thought-provoking book, "Jane Austen's Pride and Prejudice in 61 Haiku.")

Perhaps my favorite poem is his "La Traviata for Dummies." If there was ever an art form that glorified death, it is the wealth of operas in which, at the end of the final act — which can never come soon enough for me — everyone is either dead or dying. As Jim puts it so succinctly:

Foreword

Everyone deserves a happy ending, whether it's at a wedding or a funeral. The problem is — life.

By night, I write Regency-era romances. By day, I officiate at weddings and funerals as a rabbi. The two parts of my life, like this book, are oddly compatible. The feelings evoked by both life cycle events — weddings and funerals —are oddly similar. Except that there are often more laughs at funerals and more tears at weddings.

My dear friend, James W. Gaynor, has brilliantly captured this paradox in his lovely collection of poems that reflect on the human condition at the best and worst times of our lives. (And don't fall into the trap of thinking that weddings are the best!)

20 Poems Inappropriate for a Funeral

Switching from the ridiculous to the sublime, the reader will find much on which to muse in Jim's collections of poems inappropriate for funerals. As with marriage, Jim has never been dead, so his observations of this state are unsullied by actual experience. He is, however, an insightful observer of all things death-related, and so the poems in this collection have much that the reader will find of interest.

Jersey nursing homes – offi-
d long-term care facilities – at
residents have died from the
ifficulty dealing with COVID
kes you look to see if the en
is in need of change," said Al
. Andrew Cuomo said if
can't handle an infectec
eed to call the state tc
All it takes is one p
We're doing everytl

www.ingramcontent.com/pod-product-compliance
Lightning Source LLC
Chambersburg PA
CBHW041230020526
44118CB0004B/2855